Cupcake Recipes That Will Amaze You with The Flavor

Cupcake Cookbook for Experts and Newbies

BY: Allie Allen

COOK & ENJOY

Copyright 2019 Allie Allen

Copyright Notes

This book is written as an informational tool. While the author has taken every precaution to ensure the accuracy of the information provided therein, the reader is warned that they assume all risk when following the content. The author will not be held responsible for any damages that may occur as a result of the readers' actions.

The author does not give permission to reproduce this book in any form, including but not limited to: print, social media posts, electronic copies or photocopies, unless permission is expressly given in writing.

My Gift to You for Buying My Book!

I would like to extend an exclusive offer to receive free and discounted eBooks every day! This special gift is my way of saying thanks. If you fill in the subscription box below you will begin to receive special offers directly to your email.

Not only that! You will also receive notifications letting you know when an offer will expire. You will never miss a chance to get a free book! Who wouldn't want that?

Fill in the subscriber information below and get started today!

https://allie-allen.getresponsepages.com/

Table of Contents

Homemade Cupcake

Recipes

ssssssssssssssssssssssssssssssssssssssssssssssssssssssssss

Chapter 1 - Fruity Cupcake Recipes

sssssssssssssssssssssssssssssssssssssssssssssssssssssss

1) Vanilla Cupcakes with Blackberry Cream Frosting

While the vanilla cupcake portion of this recipe is tasty, it's the blackberry cream frosting that steals the show.

Makes: 24 cupcakes

Cooking Time: 55 to 65 minutes

List of Ingredients:

- 1 cup flour, all-purpose
- 1 cup flour, cake
- 1 cup granulated sugar
- ½ tsp. salt
- 1 ½ tsp. baking powder
- 1 stick unsalted butter, softened
- 2 large eggs
- ¾ cup buttermilk
- 1 ½ tsp. vanilla extract
- 3 tbsp. lemon zest

Frosting Ingredients:

- 1 tsp. vanilla extract
- 3 cups powdered sugar
- ¼ cup blackberry preserve

SSSSSSSSSSSSSSSSSSSSSSSSSSSSSSSSSSSSSSSSSSSSSSSSSSSSSSSSSSSS

Methods:

Step 1: Preheat the oven to 375-degrees. Prepare a cupcake tin by lining it with paper liners. Set the tin to the side for the moment.

Step 2: In a mixing bowl, cream the butter and the sugar together until fluffy. Beat the eggs in one at a time. Set to the side for the moment.

Step 3: In a separate mixing bowl, sift together all the dry ingredients.

Step 4: Gradually add the dry ingredients to the butter mixture, stirring constantly. Stir in the buttermilk followed by the vanilla extract.

Step 5: Fill the cupcake tin ¾ full with the batter. Place the tin in the oven and bake for 20- to 24-minutes. Remove the cupcake tin from the oven and let cool for about 10 minutes.

Step 6: Remove the cupcakes from the tin and let cool completely on a wire rack.

Step 7: Make the frosting by beating the butter with a mixer until fluffy. Once fluffy, add the powdered sugar while continuing to beat with the mixer. Add the vanilla and the blackberry preserve until well blended.

Step 8: Spread the frosting over the cooled cupcake or pipe it on using a pastry bag and frosting tip.

2) Lemon Cupcakes

If you love the flavor of lemons and want a cupcake that is bursting with fruity flavor, look no further than this refreshing recipe.

Makes: 12 cupcakes

Cooking Time: 65 minutes

List of Ingredients:

- ¾ cup cake flour
- ¾ cup flour, all-purpose
- 1/8 tsp. baking soda
- 1 tsp. baking powder
- ¼ tsp. salt
- ¾ cup granulated sugar
- ½ cup unsalted butter, softened
- 1 tbsp. lemon zest, grated finely
- 2 large egg whites
- 1 large egg
- 2 tbsp. lemon juice
- ½ cup milk

ss

Methods:

Step 1: Preheat the oven to 350-degrees. Prepare a cupcake tin by lining it with paper liners. Set the tin to the side for the moment.

Step 2: Sift the two flours together in a mixing bowl. Stir in the salt, baking soda and baking powder. Set the bowl to the side for the moment.

Step 3: Whisk together the sugar and butter before adding the lemon zest. Once the mixture is fluffy, add in the eggs, lemon juice and milk.

Step 4: Gradually mix the flour mixture into the egg mixture until they are just combined.

Step 5: Pour the batter into the tin until each opening is 2/3 cup full. Place the cupcake tin in the oven and bake for about 18 to 20 minutes. Let the cupcakes cool on a wire rack.

Step 6: Frost the cupcakes with vanilla or lemon frosting.

3) Citrus Spice Cupcake with Orange Frosting

This cupcake recipe brings a bit of the tropics to your kitchen with its orange, coconut and spice flavor.

Makes: 24 cupcakes

Cooking Time: 70 minutes

List of Ingredients:

- 2 ½ cups cake flour
- 1 tsp. baking soda
- 1 tsp. baking powder
- ¼ tsp. salt
- ¼ tsp. cloves
- ¼ tsp. nutmeg
- ½ tsp. ginger
- 1 tsp. cinnamon
- 1 ¼ cup brown sugar, packed
- ½ cup unsalted butter, softened
- 2 eggs, large
- 1 tbsp. orange liqueur
- ½ cup coconut milk
- ¼ cup juice from an orange
- ½ cup buttermilk
- ½ cup unsweetened coconut flakes
- Finely grated orange zest

Frosting Ingredients:

- 2 ounces cream cheese, softened
- 2 cups vanilla frosting from a can
- 1 tbsp. orange liqueur
- 2 tbsp. juice from an orange

sssssssssssssssssssssssssssssssssssssssssssssssssssssss

Methods:

Step 1: Preheat the oven to 350-degrees. Prepare a cupcake tin by lining it with paper liners. Set the tin to the side for the moment.

Step 2: Whisk the flour, baking soda, baking powder, salt, ginger, cloves, cinnamon and nutmeg together. Set to the side for the moment.

Step 3: Cream the butter with an electric mixture until fluffy. Add the sugar and beat until smooth. Beat in the eggs, one at a time, before adding the orange liqueur. Add the flour mixture and beat until well incorporated.

Step 5: Stir in the orange juice. Mix in the coconut milk before blending in the buttermilk. Add the coconut flakes and stir gently for several seconds.

Step 6: Fill the cupcake tin 2/3 full with the batter. Place the tin in the oven and bake for 20-minutes. Remove the cupcake tin from the oven and let cool for about 10 minutes. Remove the cupcakes from the tin and let cool completely on a wire rack.

Step 7: Make the frosting by beating the cream cheese, canned vanilla frosting, orange liqueur and orange together for about 3 minutes.

Step 8: Spread the frosting over the cooled cupcake or pipe it on using a pastry bag and frosting tip.

4) Simple Peaches and Cream Cupcakes with Peaches and Cream Frosting

The taste of peaches goes perfectly with cream and this simple and quick cupcake recipe proves just that.

Makes: 12 cupcakes

Cooking Time: 60 minutes

List of Ingredients:

- 5 ounces granulated sugar
- 5 ounces unsalted butter, softened
- 3 eggs, large
- 2 tsp. vanilla extract
- 5 ounces flour, all-purpose
- 2 tsp. baking powder
- 2 ripe peaches, skinned and diced
- Frosting List of Ingredients:
- 3 tbsp. sugar, powdered
- 2 tbsp. cream cheese, softened
- Peach syrup

sssssssssssssssssssssssssssssssssssssssssssssssssssssss

Methods:

Step 1: Step 1: Preheat the oven to 350-degrees. Prepare a cupcake tin by lining it with paper liners. Set the tin to the side for the moment.

Step 2: Mix the flour and baking powder together. Set to the side.

Step 3: Cream the butter and sugar together in a separate mixing bowl. Mix the eggs in one at a time before adding the vanilla extract. Fold in the diced peaches.

Step 4: Gradually stir the flour mixture into the butter mixture.

Step 5: Fill the cupcake tin ¾ full with the batter. Place the tin in the oven and bake for 25-minutes. Remove the cupcake tin from the oven and let cool for about 10 minutes.

Step 6: Remove the cupcakes from the tin and let cool completely on a wire rack.

Step 7: Make the frosting by whisking the powdered sugar and cream cheese together. Stir in the peach syrup a little at a time, tasting the frosting until you get the desired flavor.

Step 8: Spread the frosting over the cooled cupcake or pipe it on using a pastry bag and frosting tip.

5) Banana and Walnut Cupcake

These extra moist cupcakes are similar in taste as banana walnut bread. Frost with the Simple Cream Cheese frosting recipe to take these cupcakes to a higher level.

Makes: 12 cupcakes

Cooking Time: 60 minutes

List of Ingredients:

- ¾ cup brown sugar, packed
- ½ cup unsalted butter, softened
- 1 tsp. vanilla extract
- 2 large eggs
- 1 cup flour, all-purpose
- ½ tsp. baking soda
- 1 tsp. baking powder
- ½ tsp. nutmeg
- ¼ tsp. salt
- ½ cup ripe banana, peeled and mashed
- ½ cup sour cream
- ½ cup walnuts, finely chopped

ssssssssssssssssssssssssssssssssssssssssssssssssssssssss

Methods:

Step 1: Step 1: Preheat the oven to 350-degrees. Prepare a cupcake tin by lining it with paper liners. Set the tin to the side for the moment.

Step 2: Cream the sugar and butter together until light and fluffy. Add the vanilla and beat for about 2 to 3 minutes. Add the eggs and beat well.

Step 3: In a separate bowl, sift the flour, salt, nutmeg and baking soda together. Slowly add this mixture to the butter mixture while blending until well mixed.

Step 4: Mix in the sour cream, followed by the mashed banana and finely chopped walnuts.

Step 5: Fill the cupcake tin ¾ full with the batter. Place the tin in the oven and bake for 20-minutes. Remove the cupcake tin from the oven and let cool for about 10 minutes. Remove the cupcakes from the tin and let cool completely on a wire rack.

Step 6: Frost cooled cupcakes with your favorite cream cheese frosting.

6) Apple Pie Cupcakes with Cinnamon Frosting

Turn the traditional flavor of delicious apple pie into moist cupcakes with this yummy recipe.

Makes: 24

Cooking Time: 65 minutes

List of Ingredients:

- 2 ¼ cup flour, all purpose
- 1 tsp. cinnamon
- 2 ¼ tsp. baking powder
- ¼ tsp. salt
- 2 sticks + 2 tbsp. unsalted butter, softened
- 1 ½ cups sugar, granulated
- 4 large eggs
- 1 cup milk
- ½ tsp. vanilla extract

Topping Ingredients:

- 1/3 cup sugar, granulated
- 3 tbsp. butter, unsalted
- 3 apples, peeled and cored, sliced thinly

Frosting Ingredients:

- 1 ½ cups powdered sugar
- 3 sticks unsalted butter, softened
- ½ tsp. cinnamon

sssssssssssssssssssssssssssssssssssssssssssssssssssssss

Methods:

Step 1: Preheat the oven to 325-degrees. Prepare a cupcake tin by lining it with paper liners. Set the tin to the side for the moment.

Step 2: To make the topping, cook the apples in the butter on the stove over medium heat. Add the sugar and stir until dissolved. Let the apples cook for about 10 minutes before removing them from heat.

Step 3: While the apples are cooling, start making the cupcake by mixing the flour, salt, baking powder and cinnamon together in a small bowl. Place to the side.

Step 4: Cream the sugar and butter together until they are fluffy and let. Add the eggs and continue to beat until well incorporated. Beat in the vanilla.

Step 5: Gradually beat the flour mixture into the butter mixture until well mixed. Add the milk and continue to beat until smooth.

Step 6: Fill the cupcake tin 2/3 full with the batter. Add a bit of the apple topping on top. Place the tin in the oven and bake for 20-minutes. Remove the cupcake tin from the oven and let cool for about 10 minutes.

Step 7: Make the frosting by beating the butter until fluffy and then gradually adding the powdered sugar and cinnamon. Continue to beat for an additional 5 minutes.

Step 8: Spread the frosting over the cooled cupcake or pipe it on using a pastry bag and frosting tip.

Chapter II – Chocolate Cupcake Recipes

SSSSSSSSSSSSSSSSSSSSSSSSSSSSSSSSSSSSSSSSSSSSSSSSSSSSSSSS

7) Chocolaty Bacon Cupcakes

In recent years, the combination of chocolate and bacon has become popular and this cupcake recipe utilizes that flavor combo to create an interesting and delicious treat.

Makes: 24

Cooking Time: 40 minutes + time to cool

List of Ingredients:

- ¾ cup hot water
- 3 cups all-purpose flour
- ¾ cup unsweetened cocoa powder
- 1 tsp. baking soda
- 1 tsp. baking powder
- 1 ¼ tsp. salt
- 2 ¼ cup granulated sugar
- 4 large eggs
- 1 cup sour cream
- 1 tbsp. + 1 tsp. vanilla extract
- ¾ cup cooked bacon, crumbled

sssssssssssssssssssssssssssssssssssssssssssssssssssssssss

Methods:

Step 1: Step 1: Preheat the oven to 350-degrees. Prepare a cupcake tin by lining it with paper liners. Set the tin to the side for the moment.

Step 2: Add the hot water to a bowl and stir in the cocoa powder. Set to the side.

Step 3: In a separate bowl, sift the flour, salt, baking soda and baking powder together. Set the bowl to the side.

Step 4: Melt the butter in a small saucepan over low heat. Once melted, stir in the granulated sugar. Pour this mixture into a mixing bowl.

Step 5: Using an electric mixer, whisk the mixture together for about 5 minutes. Add the eggs and beat one at a time. Add the vanilla extract and cocoa/water mixture and whisk. Add the sour cream and flour and continue whisking until well incorporated.

Step 6: Fold the crumbled bacon by hand into the batter.

Step 7: Fill the cupcake tin ¾ full with the batter. Place the tin in the oven and bake for 20-minutes. Remove the cupcake tin from the oven and let cool for about 10 minutes.

Step 8: Remove the cupcakes from the tin and let cool completely on a wire rack.

Step 9: Frost with Maple frosting.

8) Cookie Dough Cupcakes

The added cookie dough found in the middle of this cupcake makes a tasty surprise.

Makes: 24 cupcakes

Cooking Time: 40 minutes + time to cool

List of Ingredients:

- 2 2/3 cup flour, all-purpose
- 1 tsp. baking soda
- 1 tsp. baking powder
- ¼ tsp. salt
- 3 sticks unsalted butter, softened
- 1 ½ cups brown sugar, light
- 1 cup milk
- 4 large eggs
- 2 tsp. vanilla
- Package of refrigerated cookie dough

ssssssssssssssssssssssssssssssssssssssssssssssssssssssss

Methods:

Step 1: Open the package of refrigerated cookie dough and roll into 24 small balls. Place these balls in the freezer and let chill overnight.

Step 2: Preheat the oven to 350-degrees and line the cupcake/muffin tin with cupcake liners.

Step 3: Cream the brown sugar and butter together until fluffy and light. Add the eggs, one at a time, and mix until thoroughly combined.

Step 4: In a separate bowl, mix the baking powder, baking soda, flour and salt. Gradually mix the flour mixture into the butter mixture. Add the milk and vanilla blend.

Step 5: Fill the cupcake tin ¾ full with the batter. Insert a frozen cookie dough ball from Step 1 into each batter-filled cupcake tin.

Step 6: Place the tin in the oven and bake for 20-minutes. Remove the cupcake tin from the oven and let cool for about 10 minutes. Remove the cupcakes from the tin and let cool completely on a wire rack.

Step 7: Frost the cooled cupcake with chocolate chip frosting.

9) Mocha Cupcakes

This cupcake recipe is prefect for coffee-lovers or anyone who likes that traditional coffee taste and pairs well with the espresso frosting.

Makes: 12 cupcakes

Cooking Time: 40 minutes + time to cool

List of Ingredients:

- ½ cup coffee, strongly brewed
- 1 ½ tsp. espresso powder
- ½ cup milk, whole
- 1 tsp. vanilla extract
- ½ tsp. baking soda
- ¼ tsp. salt
- 1 tsp. baking powder
- 1 1/3 cup flour, all-purpose
- 1/3 cup unsweetened cocoa powder
- ½ cup granulated sugar
- ½ cup brown sugar, packed
- ½ cup unsalted butter, softened
- 1 large egg

SSSSSSSSSSSSSSSSSSSSSSSSSSSSSSSSSSSSSSSSSSSSSSSSSSSSSSSS

Methods:

Step 1: Preheat the oven to 350-degrees. Prepare a cupcake tin by lining it with paper liners. Set the tin to the side for the moment.

Step 2: Pour the strongly brewed coffee into a large cup. Stir in the espresso powder and let cool. Once cooled, stir in the whole milk and the vanilla extract.

Step 3: In a mixing bowl, whisk together the flour, baking powder, baking soda and salt. Stir in the cocoa.

Step 4: In a separate mixing bowl, cream the butter, granulated sugar and brown sugar together. Beat in the egg. Slowly stir the flour mixture into the butter mixture. Add the coffee mixture and beat until well blended.

Step 5: Fill the cupcake tin ¾ full with the batter. Place in the preheated oven and bake for 20 minutes. Remove the tin from the oven and let cool for about 10 minutes before removing the cupcakes from the tin and allowing them to cool completely on a wire rack.

Step 6: Frost with your favorite frosting.

10) Cookies and Cream Cupcake

Oreos are the famous ingredient in this recipe that gives the cupcakes and frosting the perfect cookies and cream flavor.

Makes: 12 cupcakes

Cooking Time: 40 minutes + extra for cooling

List of Ingredients:

- 1 ¾ cups flour, all-purpose
- 2 cups granulated sugar
- ¾ cups unsweetened cocoa powder
- 1 ½ tsp. baking soda
- 1 ½ tsp. baking powder
- 1 tsp. salt
- 1 cup milk
- 2 large eggs
- ½ cup vegetable oil
- 1 cup boiling water
- 2 tsp. vanilla extract

sss

Methods:

Step 1: Preheat the oven to 350-degrees. Prepare a cupcake tin by lining it with paper liners. Set the tin to the side for the moment.

Step 2: Combine the flour, sugar, cocoa, baking powder, baking soda and salt together in a bowl. Set to the side.

Step 3: Use an electric mixer to whisk together the milk, oil, eggs and vanilla for about 2 minutes.

Step 4: Slowly add the flour mixture to the egg mixture while whisking constantly. Add the boiling water and whisk once again until thoroughly combined.

Step 5: Fill the cupcake tin ¾ full with the batter. Place the tin in the oven and bake for 25-minutes. Remove the cupcake tin from the oven and let cool for about 10 minutes.

Step 6: Frost the cupcakes with cookies and cream frosting.

11) Cardamom Cupcakes

The chocolate cream cheese frosting really brings this simple yet delicious cupcake together.

Makes: 12 cupcakes

Cooking Time: 40 minutes + time to cool

List of Ingredients:

- ¾ cup flour, all-purpose
- 1/3 cup Dutch-process cocoa powder
- ¾ cup granulated sugar
- ¼ tsp. salt
- 1 tsp. baking powder
- ¼ tsp. baking soda
- ½ tsp. cardamom
- ¼ tsp. cinnamon
- 1/3 cup buttermilk
- 1 tsp. vanilla
- 1 large egg
- 1 egg white
- 4 tbsp. unsalted butter, melted

- 1 ounce dark chocolate, melted

sssssssssssssssssssssssssssssssssssssssssssssssssssssss

Methods:

Step 1: Preheat the oven to 350-degrees. Prepare a cupcake tin by lining it with paper liners. Set the tin to the side for the moment.

Step 2: In a large mixing bowl, whisk together the baking powder, baking soda, salt, cardamom, cocoa, flour, sugar and cinnamon together. Set to the side.

Step 3: Whisk together the egg white, egg, buttermilk, vanilla, butter and chocolate until thoroughly combined.

Step 4: Slowly pour the flour mixture into the butter mixture while stirring constantly. Continue until the batter is well mixed.

Step 5: Fill the cupcake tin ¾ full with the batter. Place the tin in the oven and bake for 20-minutes. Remove the cupcake tin from the oven and let cool for about 10 minutes.

Step 6: Remove the cupcakes from the tin and let cool completely on a wire rack.

Chapter III – Candy and Beverage Cupcake Recipes

SSSSSSSSSSSSSSSSSSSSSSSSSSSSSSSSSSSSSSSSSSSSSSSSSSSSSSSSS

12) KitKat Cupcakes with KitKat Frosting

Made to taste like a KitKat bar, this delicious cupcake recipe has the secret ingredient of coffee to give it a unique taste.

Makes: 12 cupcakes

Cooking Time: 65 minutes

List of Ingredients:

- 1 cup granulated sugar
- 1 cup flour, all-purpose
- 1/3 cup cocoa powder, unsweetened
- ½ tsp. baking powder
- 1 tsp. baking soda
- ½ tsp. salt
- 1 large egg
- ½ cup strongly brewed coffee, hot
- ½ cup buttermilk, room temperature
- ¼ cup vegetable oil
- 1 ½ tsp. vanilla extract

Frosting Ingredients:

- 2 sticks unsalted butter, softened
- 3 ½ cups powdered sugar
- 2 tsp. vanilla extract
- 2 ½ tbsp. heavy cream
- Pinch of salt
- 7 snack size KitKat bars, finely chopped

sssssssssssssssssssssssssssssssssssssssssssssssssssssssssssss

Methods:

Step 1: Preheat the oven to 350-degrees. Prepare a cupcake tin by lining it with paper liners. Set the tin to the side for the moment.

Step 2: Mix all the dry ingredients together in a medium-sized mixing bowl. Set to the side.

Step 3: In a second mixing bowl, whisk all the wet ingredients together. When mixing, try not to let the hot coffee cook the egg.

Step 4: Gradually pour the dry mixture into the wet mixture stirring until smooth.

Step 5: Fill the cupcake tin ¾ full with the batter. Place the tin in the oven and bake for 12- to 15-minutes. Remove the cupcake tin from the oven and let cool for about 10 minutes. Remove the cupcakes from the tin and let cool completely on a wire rack.

Step 6: Make the frosting by whipping the butter for about 2 minutes. Whip in the salt, vanilla extract, heavy cream and powdered sugar until smooth. Fold in the chopped KitKat bars.

Step 7: Spread the frosting over the cooled cupcake or pipe it on using a pastry bag and frosting tip.

13) Snickers Cupcake with Peanut Butter and Chocolate Frosting

Who doesn't love Snickers? The chocolate, caramel and nuts are delicious and make a yummy cupcake!

Makes: 12 cupcakes

Cooking Time: 65 minutes

List of Ingredients:

- 1 ½ cup flour, all-purpose
- 1 cup cocoa powder, unsweetened
- 1 ½ tsp. baking powder
- 1 tsp. baking soda
- ½ tsp. salt
- 4 large eggs
- 1 cup brown sugar, packed
- 1 cup granulated sugar
- 2/3 cup vegetable oil
- 1 cup milk

- 1 tsp. vanilla extract

Frosting Ingredients:

- ½ cup creamy peanut butter
- ¾ cup unsalted butter, softened
- ½ cup cocoa powder, unsweetened
- 2 tsp. vanilla extract
- 3 ½ cups powdered sugar
- 2 ½ tbsp. milk
- Mini Snickers bars, unwrapped
- Caramel Sauce

sssssssssssssssssssssssssssssssssssssssssssssssssssssssss

Methods:

Step 1: Preheat the oven to 350-degrees. Prepare a cupcake tin by lining it with paper liners. Set the tin to the side for the moment.

Step 2: Mix the flour, cocoa, baking powder, baking soda and salt together. Set to the side.

Step 3: In a large mixing bowl, mix the granulated sugar, brown sugar, eggs, oil, milk and vanilla together until smooth.

Step 4: Gradually add the flour mixture to the sugar mixture while stirring until well combined.

Step 5: Fill the cupcake tin 2/3 full with the batter. Place the tin in the oven and bake for 20-minutes. Remove the cupcake tin from the oven and let cool for about 10 minutes. Remove the cupcakes from the tin and let cool completely on a wire rack.

Step 6: Make the frosting by beating the peanut butter and the butter together until smooth. Stir in the vanilla, milk and cocoa powder. Add the powdered sugar and mix until smooth.

Step 7: Spread the frosting over the cooled cupcake or pipe it on using a pastry bag and frosting tip. Top each cupcake with a mini Snickers bar and drizzle caramel sauce over the top.

14) Root Beer Cupcakes with Bourbon Cream Frosting

If you love root beer then you're going to flip for this cupcake recipe, which uses root beer to flavor it.

Makes: 12 cupcakes

Cooking Time: 70 minutes

List of Ingredients:

- ¼ cup unsalted butter, softened
- 1 ½ cups root beer
- ¾ cups cocoa, unsweetened
- 2 cups packed brown sugar
- 2 large eggs
- ¾ cups sour cream
- 1 tsp. vanilla extract
- 2 cups flour, all-purpose
- 2 ½ tsp. baking soda

Frosting Ingredients:

- ½ cup shortening
- ½ cup softened butter, unsalted
- ½ tsp. salt
- 4 cups powdered sugar
- 4 tbsp. Bourbon Cream liquor

ssssssssssssssssssssssssssssssssssssssssssssssssssssssssss

Methods:

Step 1: Preheat the oven to 325-degrees. Prepare a cupcake tin by lining it with paper liners. Set the tin to the side for the moment.

Step 2: In a saucepan over medium heat, melt the butter. Remove from heat and then stir in the root beer until well mixed. Set to the side for the moment.

Step 3: In a mixing bowl, whisk the eggs, sour cream and vanilla together. Pour the root beer mixture into the bowl and whisk until combined. Pour in the sugar and cocoa and stir.

Step 4: In another bowl, shift together the baking soda and flour. Gradually pour into the root bear mixture and whisk until well incorporated.

Step 5: Fill the cupcake tin ¾ full with the batter. Place the tin in the oven and bake for 15 to 18-minutes. Remove the cupcake tin from the oven and let cool for about 10 minutes. Remove the cupcakes from the tin and let cool completely on a wire rack.

Step 6: Make the frosting by mixing the shortening with the butter for about 10 minutes. Add the powdered sugar and mix. Stir in the salt and the bourbon cream.

Step 7: Spread the frosting over the cooled cupcake or pipe it on using a pastry bag and frosting tip.

15) Peppermint Patty Cupcakes with Mint Frosting

If you like the refreshing taste of mint then you're going to love this minty cupcake recipe.

Makes: 12 cupcakes

Cooking Time: 55 to 65 minutes

List of Ingredients:

- 2/3 cup unsweetened cocoa powder
- 1 tsp. baking soda
- 1 cup boiling water
- ½ cup unsalted butter, melted
- 5 tbsp. oil, vegetable
- 2 tsp. vanilla extract
- 1 ½ cup granulated sugar
- ½ tsp. salt
- ½ cup heavy cream
- 4 large eggs
- 1 ½ cup flour, all-purpose
- 6 Peppermint Patties, unwrapped and halved

Frosting Ingredients:

- 2 tsp. mint extract
- 1 ½ cups unsalted butter, softened
- 2 tsp. vanilla extract
- 1 tbsp. milk
- 5 cups powdered sugar
- 1 cup mini chocolate chips
- Food coloring, green

sssssssssssssssssssssssssssssssssssssssssssssssssssssss

Methods:

Step 1: Preheat the oven to 350-degrees. Prepare a cupcake tin by lining it with paper liners. Set the tin to the side for the moment.

Step 2: Mix the baking soda and cocoa powder together in a large mixing bowl. Add the boiling water and stir until combined.

Step 3: In a separate bowl, cream the butter and sugar together. Add the oil, eggs, salt and vanilla and stir. Stir in the mixture from Step 2 and the cream.

Step 4: Slowly add the flour the mixture and stir until it is just combined. Avoid over stirring.

Step 5: Fill the cupcake tin ¾ full with the batter. Place the tin in the oven and bake for 20-minutes. Remove the cupcake tin from the oven and let cool for about 10 minutes. Remove the cupcakes from the tin and let cool completely on a wire rack.

Step 6: Make the frosting by mixing the butter until fluffy and then stirring in the vanilla and mint extracts. Slowly mix in the powdered sugar and the milk. Add one drop of food coloring at a time, stirring after each drop, until you achieve the desired green color. Carefully fold the chocolate chips into the frosting.

Step 7: Spread the frosting over the cooled cupcake or pipe it on using a pastry bag and frosting tip. Top each cupcake with half a Peppermint Patty.

Chapter IV – Frosting Recipes

ssssssssssssssssssssssssssssssssssssssssssssssssssssss

16) Triple Berry Buttercream Frosting

Despite its rather extensive sounding name, this buttercream frosting recipe is easy to throw together in a few minutes and will bring some fruity fun to any cupcake.

Makes: Frosts 24 cupcakes

Cooking Time: 15 to 20 minutes

List of Ingredients:

- 2 sticks unsalted butter, softened
- 1 tsp. vanilla extract
- 3 cups powdered sugar
- 1 tbsp. raspberry preserve
- 1 tbsp. blackberry preserve
- 1 tbsp. strawberry preserve

SSSSSSSSSSSSSSSSSSSSSSSSSSSSSSSSSSSSSSSSSSSSSSSSSSSS

Methods:

Step 1: Using a mixer, cream the unsalted butter for a few minutes until it becomes fluffy.

Step 2: Gradually add the powdered sugar while constantly beating the two ingredients together.

Step 3: Add in the vanilla and mix until well incorporated. Stir in all three berry preserves until thoroughly combined.

Step 3: Spread the frosting over the cooled cupcake or pipe it on using a pastry bag and frosting tip.

17) Espresso Frosting

This frosting recipe works well on mocha, chocolate or vanilla cupcakes.

Makes: Frosts 12 cupcakes

Cooking Time: 20 minutes

List of Ingredients:

- 1 ½ tsp. vanilla extract
- 1 ½ tsp. espresso powder
- 2 ½ cups powdered sugar
- 1 cup unsalted butter, softened

sssssssssssssssssssssssssssssssssssssssssssssssssssssssss

Methods:

Step 1: Mix the espresso with the vanilla in a cup. Set to the side.

Step 2: Whisk the butter for about 5 minutes before slowly adding the sugar. Continue mixing for a few minutes before adding the vanilla/espresso mixture. Continue to whisk until the frosting has a fluffy consistency.

Step 3: Spread the frosting over the cooled cupcake or pipe it on using a pastry bag and frosting tip.

18) Coconut Pecan Frosting

While it can be used on any cupcake you want, this coconut pecan frosting works the best on German chocolate cupcakes.

Makes: Frosts 12 cupcakes

Cooking Time: 25 minutes

List of Ingredients:

- 3 large egg yolks
- 1 can condensed milk, sweetened
- ½ cup unsalted butter, softened
- 1 tsp. vanilla extract
- 1 cup finely chopped pecans
- 1 cup shredded coconut, sweetened

ssssssssssssssssssssssssssssssssssssssssssssssssssssss

Methods:

Step 1: Heat the butter, egg yolks and milk in a saucepan until it reaches 165-degrees. Make sure to stir the mixture constantly during the heating process.

Step 2: Remove the mixture from heat and stir in the vanilla extract, pecans and coconut. Let cool before continuing.

Step 3: Spread the frosting over the cooled cupcake or pipe it on using a pastry bag and frosting tip.

19) Chocolate Cream Cheese Frosting

Use this recipe on just about any cupcake where you want to add a bit of chocolate flavoring.

Makes: Frosts 12 cupcakes

Cooking Time: 20 minutes

List of Ingredients:

- 1 stick unsalted butter, softened
- 8 ounces cream cheese, softened
- 2 tsp. vanilla
- 3 cups powdered sugar
- ½ cup Dutch-processed cocoa powder

SSSSSSSSSSSSSSSSSSSSSSSSSSSSSSSSSSSSSSSSSSSSSSSSSSSSSSSS

Methods:

Step 1: Make the frosting by creaming the butter and the cream cheese together. Add the vanilla and stir. Gradually pour in the powdered sugar and cocoa and continue to mix until the frosting is fluffy.

Step 2: Spread the frosting over the cooled cupcake or pipe it on using a pastry bag and frosting tip.

20) Mango Buttercream Frosting

This citrusy frosting recipe can turn a simple vanilla or white cupcake into a tropical dessert in a matter of minutes.

Makes: Frosts 12 cupcakes

Cooking Time: 15 minutes

List of Ingredients:

- 1/8 cup milk
- ½ cup softened butter, salted
- ½ tsp. vanilla extract
- 3 cups powdered sugar
- 1 tbsp. lime juice
- ½ cup mashed mango

SSSSSSSSSSSSSSSSSSSSSSSSSSSSSSSSSSSSSSSSSSSSSSSSSSSSSSSSS

Methods:

Step 1: In a mixing bowl, cream the butter until it is fluffy. Add the vanilla extract, lime juice and mashed mango.

Step 2: Slowly add the powdered sugar and the milk, mixing constantly during the process and alternating between the two.

Step 3: Spread the frosting over the cooled cupcake or pipe it on using a pastry bag and frosting tip.

21) Maple Frosting

For an unusual yet extremely delicious experience, par this frosting with Bacon cupcakes.

Makes: Frosts 24 cupcakes

Cooking Time: 25 minutes

List of Ingredients:

- 2 sticks unsalted butter, softened
- 1 tsp. vanilla
- 1 pound powdered sugar
- 1 tsp. salt
- 1/3 cup real maple syrup + extra to drizzle

sssssssssssssssssssssssssssssssssssssssssssssssssssssss

Methods:

Step 1: Add the butter into a mixing bowl and whisking for several minutes. Add the vanilla, maple syrup and salt and continue to whisk.

Step 2: Gradually add the powdered sugar while whisking constantly until the frosting is fluffy.

Step 3: Spread the frosting over the cooled cupcake or pipe it on using a pastry bag and frosting tip. Sprinkle some crumbled bacon over the top of the frosting, followed by a drizzle of maple syrup.

22) Simple Cream Cheese Frosting

This simple frosting recipe can be used on a wide array of cupcakes.

Makes: Frosts 12 cupcakes

Cooking Time: 20 minutes

List of Ingredients:

- 1 cup cream cheese, room temperature
- 1 cup powdered sugar
- ½ tsp. vanilla extract
- 1 tbsp. heavy cream

ssssssssssssssssssssssssssssssssssssssssssssssssssssssss

Methods:

Step 1: Make the cream cheese frosting by mixing the cream cheese with the powdered sugar until smooth.

Step 2: Add the vanilla and heavy cream and continue to beat until well incorporated.

Step 3: Spread the frosting over the cooled cupcake or pipe it on using a pastry bag and frosting tip.

23) Cookies and Cream Frosting

Use this recipe to frost the cookies and cream cupcakes.

Makes: Frosts 12 cupcakes

Cooking Time: 25 minutes

List of Ingredients:

- 4 tbsp. powdered sugar
- 2 cups whipping cream
- 1 tsp. vanilla extract
- 12 Oreo sandwich cookies, crushed
- 12 Oreos halved, for garnish

SSSSSSSSSSSSSSSSSSSSSSSSSSSSSSSSSSSSSSSSSSSSSSSSSSSSSSSS

Methods:

Step 1: Mix the sugar, whipping cream and vanilla together using an electric mixer. Whisk until stiff peaks begin to form. Add the crushed Oreos and fold in by hand.

Step 2: Spread the frosting over the cooled cupcake or pipe it on using a pastry bag and frosting tip.

24) Creamy Lemon Butter Frosting

This refreshing frosting recipes is a great addition to the Lemon cupcake recipe found in this book.

Makes: Frosts 12 cupcakes

Cooking Time: 20 to 25 minutes

List of Ingredients:

- 1 cup unsalted butter, softened
- 1 ½ cup powdered sugar
- 1 ½ tsp. lemon zest
- 1 tbsp. heavy cream
- 1 tbsp. lemon juice
- ¼ tsp. lemon extract
- ½ tsp. vanilla extract

sssssssssssssssssssssssssssssssssssssssssssssssssssssss

Methods:

Step 1: Whip the butter with the lemon zest until fluffy. Add the powdered sugar slowly and continue to whip.

Step 2: Pour the cream, lemon juice, lemon extract and vanilla extract into the bowl. Continue whipping until well combined.

Step 3: Spread the frosting over the cooled cupcake or pipe it on using a pastry bag and frosting tip. Top each cupcake with a sprinkle of lemon zest.

25) Chocolate Chip Frosting

This frosting recipes works best when paired with the Cookie Dough cupcakes.

Makes: Frosts 24 cupcakes

Cooking Time: 20 minutes

List of Ingredients:

- 3 sticks unsalted butter, softened
- ¾ cup brown sugar, packed
- 3 ½ cups powdered sugar
- 2 tbsp. milk
- ½ tsp. salt
- 1 tsp. vanilla
- Package mini chocolate chips (for garnish)

ssssssssssssssssssssssssssssssssssssssssssssssssssssssss

Methods:

Step 1: Cream the brown sugar and butter together until fluffy. Add the powdered sugar and mix until smooth. Blend in the vanilla, milk and salt.

Step 2: Spread the frosting over the cooled cupcake or pipe it on using a pastry bag and frosting tip. Sprinkle the mini chocolate chips over top the frosting.

About the Author

Allie Allen developed her passion for the culinary arts at the tender age of five when she would help her mother cook for their large family of 8. Even back then, her family knew this would be more than a hobby for the young Allie and when she graduated from high school, she applied to cooking school in London. It had always been a dream of the young chef to study with some of Europe's best and she made it happen by attending the Chef Academy of London.

After graduation, Allie decided to bring her skills back to North America and open up her own restaurant. After 10 successful years as head chef and owner, she decided to sell her business and pursue other career avenues. This monumental decision led Allie to her true calling, teaching. She also started to write e-books for her students to study at home for practice. She is now the proud author of several e-books and gives private and semi-private cooking lessons to a range of students at all levels of experience.

Stay tuned for more from this dynamic chef and teacher when she releases more informative e-books on cooking and baking in the near future. Her work is infused with stores and anecdotes you will love!

Author's Afterthoughts

I can't tell you how grateful I am that you decided to read my book. My most heartfelt thanks that you took time out of your life to choose my work and I hope you find benefit within these pages.

There are so many books available today that offer similar content so that makes it even more humbling that you decided to buying mine.

Tell me what you thought! I am eager to hear your opinion and ideas on what you read as are others who are looking for a good book to buy. Leave a review on Amazon.com so others can benefit from your wisdom!

With much thanks,

Allie Allen

Made in the USA
Coppell, TX
22 August 2021